TAKING CARE OF YOUR

GUINEA PIG

Contents

Introducing pets

People like to keep pets. They can be an interesting part of our lives. It has been proved that the company of a pet is often helpful to somebody who is alone or unwell.

By caring for and watching a pet, we can find out how other creatures use the world. But there are a few very important things to think about when you decide to have a pet.

▽ The Abyssinian guinea pig is one of the most popular breeds of guinea pig. It is quite an active creature but is unlikely to struggle or bite if handled properly.

Points to remember

You must remember that a pet is not a toy, which you can put away and forget, but a living creature like yourself. Like you it can be contented or afraid. It must have food, drink and a safe, warm place to sleep. Like you, it needs exercise and play.

If you remember these things. Your pet will trust you and be happy with you.

▽ Guinea pigs can give a lot of pleasure as pets, especially to someone who is disabled. Great care should be taken to avoid dropping the animals while you are handling them.

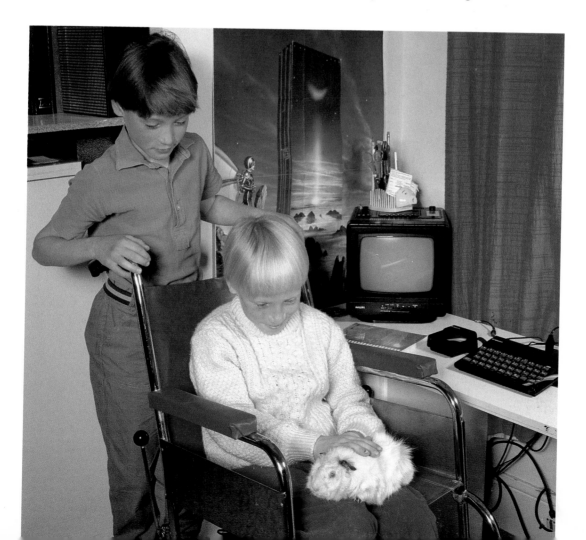

Good pets

Guinea pigs are among the most gentle of small animals, so they make very good pets but they can be easily frightened.

They do not take up much space, nor do they eat a great deal of food.

Guinea pigs are not expensive to buy and they are not noisy animals. If properly looked after they are free of bad odors, so it is quite possible to keep them indoors.

▽ Guinea pigs can become very tame. They live longer than many small creatures, normally surviving for at least three years and sometimes for a good deal longer.

If you decide to keep a guinea pig you must be sure that everyone in your household agrees to your having the pet. You must also be certain that you have enough space to keep it.

Guinea pigs are very sensitive to cold weather, especially if it is also damp, so you must keep them in a place which is fairly warm and draft free. Do not put them in a garage, as the fumes from cars are very bad for them. There will be expenses in keeping the animal because you will need a cage, bedding and food.

△ If possible, it is good to keep your guinea pig indoors, so that it is warm and comfortable.

▽ Your guinea pig should be let out to play and explore sometimes, but be very careful not to let cats or dogs near it.

Guinea pigs belong to a big group of animals called rodents. They have only two front or incisor teeth in the upper jaw and two in the lower jaw.

These teeth grow continuously and act like chisels to cut and nibble hard food which wears the teeth down, so they do not become too long.

Guinea pigs are mainly active in the daytime and have good eyesight, hearing and sense of smell to alert them to danger from hunting animals.

△ Peruvian guinea pigs are the best known of the long-haired breeds. Their hair falls forward over the face.

The Sheltie is another long-haired breed but is different in that the hair falls back and leaves the face and head clear.

Many varieties of guinea pig have been bred. Although there are many colors to choose from, the coat may be of three main types: smooth short-haired, rough-haired or rosetted and long-haired.

Short-haired guinea pigs are easy to groom and keep clean. Abyssinian or rosetted guinea pigs are almost as easy to care for. Long-haired breeds are difficult to look after, as the hair grows continually.

▽ The coat of the Abyssinian guinea pig should be about 1½in (4cm) long and rough to touch. The color of this one is referred to as 'roan.'

△ Most pet guinea pigs are of the short-haired type, which are easy to care for. Many, like this one are a mixture of colors.

The Abyssinian is the commonest of the rough-haired breeds of guinea pig. Their hair grows against the grain from a series of points down their back and sides, giving clearly marked rosettes. Where these join, they form ridges down the back and across the shoulders.

Another rough-haired breed is the crested guinea pig, in which the coat is mainly short but there is a tuft of long hair on the top of the head. A fairly new breed is the Rex guinea pig, which has fairly short, wiry hair, which sticks out from the animal's body.

▽ A Rex agouti guinea pig has stiff looking, speckled fur.

△ White and other pale colored guinea pigs may have pink eyes. Those with darker colored fur rarely do so.

Whatever its coat type, a purebred guinea pig may be one of a large variety of colors. Some, which are the same color all over, are referred to as self colored. You may find a self black which has glossy black fur, with each hair entirely black.

All other breeds are called non selfs. They may be banded in black or brown and white. The Himalayan guinea pig is born pure white, but as it grows, its face, ears and feet become dark colored.

Agouti guinea pigs look speckled, for each hair has bands of two different colors on it.

▽ The Dalmatian guinea pig is a smooth-coated breed in which the white fur is marked with dark spots, like the coat of a Dalmatian dog.

△ The dark fur of a chocolate and white colored guinea pig shows the shine on the coat of a really healthy animal.

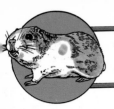

△ You may have parents or friends who can help you to make a cage for your guinea pig, but if not, you will find that most pet stores sell suitable cages.

You must decide whether to have one guinea pig or two. Guinea pigs like company, but if there is enough room to keep your pet in the house so that it will see everything that goes on and you have plenty of time to play with it, it should not be too unhappy on its own.

But if you have to keep your pets outside the house, it is far kinder to get two, so that they can keep each other company.

The size of your cage will depend on whether you intend to keep one guinea pig or two. A cage with the minimum measurements of 48in (120cm) long, 24in (60cm) wide and 20in (50cm) high is big enough for two animals. It should be made of hard wood and wire mesh (as a window only) and should include a darkened bedroom area.

You will also need food bowls, which should be fairly heavy as guinea pigs can overturn light ones. Water is best put in a drip-feed water bottle which can be attached to the wire of the cage.

Wood shavings are suitable for covering the floor of the main cage and hay can be used for the rest area.

△ The sort of bowls that are sold for food and water for small dogs are quite heavy and are therefore difficult for guinea pigs to overturn.

▽ A temporary run can be made with planks securely held with bricks. You should stay with your guinea pig if there is no mesh covering, as it may be in danger from cats or dogs.

Choosing a guinea pig

Most pet shops stock guinea pigs, so you will be able to choose the ones you want. Ask the dealer for young ones, preferably not more than eight weeks old. At this age they will be very easy to tame. If you get guinea pigs that are much older, they will probably be very suspicious of anything which is strange to them.

▽ Nowadays many pet shops will not sell animals to children on their own, so make sure that you go with an adult when you want to choose your guinea pigs. The dealer will help by showing you the animals that are in stock.

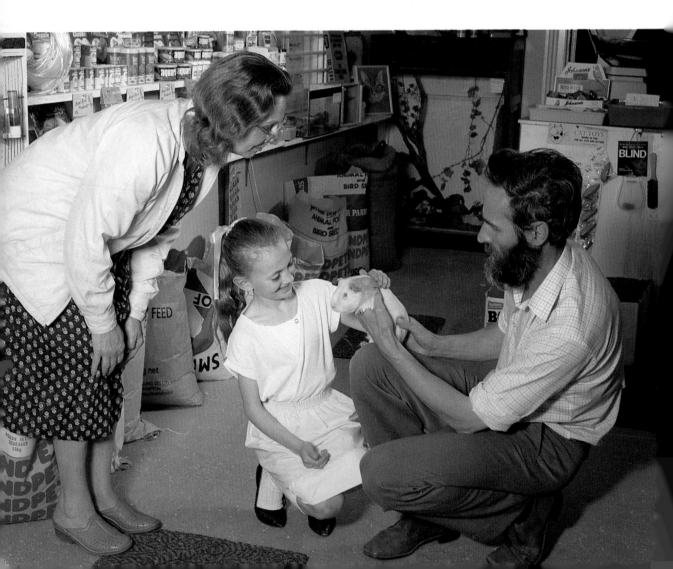

It is better to get two female guinea pigs as two males will probably fight a lot. Don't put a male and female together as they will breed very easily and you will have to find homes for the babies.

Make certain that the animals you get are healthy. A healthy guinea pig's coat is in good condition, with no bald patches or sores. If it is a short-haired variety the fur should be smooth and shiny. Look for bright eyes and clean noses, mouths and rear ends.

Choose animals that seem lively, not any that are cowering in the corner. Healthy guinea pigs make very good pets – sickly ones can never do so.

△ A guinea pig like this one, with its sparkling eyes and shiny coat, would make a very good pet.

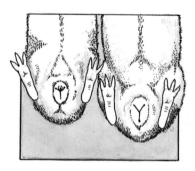

△ It is quite difficult to tell the sex of young guinea pigs. Look at the underside of the animal. If it is like the one on the left above, it is a male. If it is like the one on the right, it is a female.

15

The pet store will probably provide you with a carrying box to take your pet home in.

The box should not be too small so that the animal cannot move, but neither should it be too large. The box should have air holes in the top of it. Put soft hay in it to cushion the animal on its way home.

▽ Traveling boxes for guinea pigs can be of wood or cardboard. The one here has some bedding in it and a mesh-covered air vent.

When you are home, put your guinea pig gently into the cage. However much you want to play with it, do not do so yet. Let it settle down first.

You must learn to pick up and carry your guinea pig safely. Tempt it to come to you with a little fresh grass or a sunflower seed.

Stroke it gently and slip one hand underneath it and put the other hand over its shoulders, so that it cannot wriggle and fall. Be careful never to drop it or let it fall from its cage or a table, as it might be injured or even killed.

△ When you pick up a guinea pig it should feel secure, as though it is standing on your hand. It will do this if you are supporting its rear end and hind legs properly. Never squeeze it, or you will frighten it.

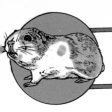

Feeding your guinea pig

Guinea pigs are herbivores, which means that they eat only vegetable food. The total amount that you should give to an adult guinea pig should be about 8oz (250g) a day. This may seem a lot for a small animal but a lot of plant food is fiber which is not completely digested.

Find out what your guinea pig has been fed on and how much it eats, as a young one will not need so much as one that is fully grown.

△ A week's supply of dry food will not cost you very much. Remember to make sure that the guinea pig always has plenty of water to drink.

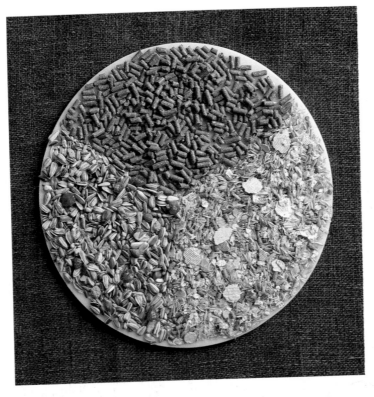

◁ Here is a selection of guinea pig food: a typical guinea pig mix, pellets and some treats of sunflower seeds, berries and flakes.

Guinea pigs should be fed twice a day at regular times. The first meal, in the morning, should consist of dry food and a handful of hay. The dry food can be crushed oats or a guinea pig food mix.

You can make this mix with pellets, grains, seeds and nuts. If you have only one or two animals it is better to buy food in packages, which will not go stale so easily.

A tablespoonful of dry food should be enough but if your guinea pig finishes its meal quickly, give it a little more. You won't do it any harm, as it won't overeat.

▽ The hay is most important. Not only for its food value but because the leaves and stems of the grass from which it is made are sufficiently tough to keep the guinea pig's teeth worn down to the right length. If hay is unavailable a small piece of hard wood will help the animal's teeth.

Guinea pigs are unusual among animals. Like human beings they cannot make vitamin C for themselves. This is why foods high in vitamin C must be supplied. Because of this, your pet's meal in the early evening, should consist of raw green vegetables, fruit, carrot or beetroots. Your guinea pig will not readily eat wilted greens or old potato peelings and if you give it these it will almost certainly become ill. It needs variety in this part of its diet and some of the raw fruit and vegetables that you eat will be best for it.

△ Lettuce, spinach, carrots, beets and cabbage are all vegetables that your guinea pig will enjoy. Sometimes, for a treat, you can give it a piece of apple or some other fruit.

If you have a garden you can grow some vegetables for your guinea pig. If you don't have a garden you should be able to find some wild food that would suit it. Grasses, clover and dandelion leaves are all good food. Be very careful not to take them from any place that has been sprayed with insecticides or weed killers as they could be poisonous.

Do not gather plants for animals near to a big road, for the fumes from the traffic may be poisonous and could get into the plants. Make sure that you know which plants you are picking and only take those, such as grasses, that you can identify.

△ The most important of the wild plants that you can collect for your guinea pig are grasses. Dandelions and clover are also very good.

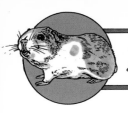

A summer ark

If you have a garden with a lawn which does not have a lot of weedkiller or fertilizer on it, your guinea pig will enjoy being outside during the summer-time.

A guinea pig ark looks a bit like an overturned boat, but it is made like this so that rain will run easily off the roof. It should be in two parts: a box-like area made of wood covered with roofing felt and a wooden frame supporting a wire cage.

▽ The materials for making an ark are not very expensive, but you will probably need the help of an adult to saw the wood and to hammer in nails and staples to make it secure.

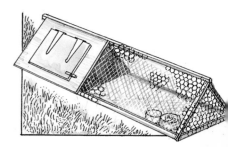

The solid part should be a few inches off the ground, so that no damp can penetrate at night. You should be able to open it so that you can clean it out. Even during the summertime there should be plenty of hay in the sleeping quarters, to keep the animals warm and because they must have some to eat.

The wire-covered part of the ark should be about two yards long so that the guinea pigs can use it as a run.

Every few days you can move the ark from one place to another so that your pets have fresh grazing. If the grass is good they will need less raw greens, but they should still have some, as well as the dry food and water.

△ An ark like this makes an ideal home for a guinea pig during the summer-time but it must have company if it is to be out for long periods.

▷ Guinea pigs should not be left for long in an open pen of this kind, although they will probably enjoy being in it as a change from an indoor cage.

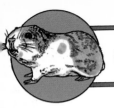

Guinea pigs are very clean animals. They tend to use the same area of the cage as a lavatory, so it is easy to remove any droppings or dirty bedding daily.

Clean out the cage once a week. Remove and replace bedding and peat or wood shavings. (Do not use sawdust for bedding, since this can cause eye trouble and breathing problems with guinea pigs.)

△ You should set some time aside each week for a thorough clean out of your guinea pig's cage. Use a scraper to make certain that you have removed all of the old bedding.

Several times a year you should thoroughly clean the cage, scrubbing it out well with disinfectant. But remember to rinse well and let it dry out completely before you return the guinea pig to it.

24

Guinea pigs groom themselves by scratching and rubbing their faces with their front paws. Short haired varieties need little help in keeping clean, although grooming them with a soft baby brush helps to give their coats an extra shine.

Long coated guinea pigs need careful brushing every day with a fairly soft brush. You may bathe your guinea pig if it is dirty using warm water and a very mild baby shampoo. Only do this in a warm place and make certain that the animal is completely dry before you put it back in its cage.

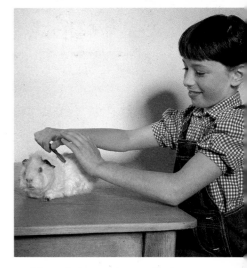

△ Abyssinian guinea pigs can be groomed with a toothbrush.

▽ Brushing removes loose hair and scurf and helps to keep the coat healthy.

Guinea pig health

If you suspect that your guinea pig is ill or that something may be wrong, you should take it to the vet as soon as possible. A vet will deal with most ailments in their early stages.

Guinea pigs can suffer very much from stress and this can turn a simple illness into a fatal one, if it is not dealt with in time. This is specially so with some skin trouble, which may be caused by tiny burrowing mites.

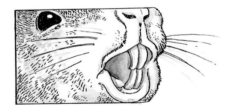

△ Guinea pigs' teeth may get broken if two adults fight, but more usually tooth trouble is caused because they grow too long.

▽ Cutting the teeth to the right length, so that the animal can chew its food again, is a job for the vet.

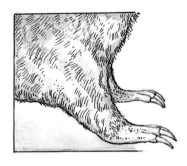

▷ If they are not kept short, guinea pigs' claws can grow until the animal is almost crippled and has difficulty in walking. Your vet will show you how to keep them trim.

△ Guinea pigs with a mite infection scratch themselves and may develop bald patches where they have lost fur. The vet can treat this condition if the animal is taken to him in time.

If you look after your guinea pig well, it will probably remain healthy throughout its life but you can help. Keep your guinea pig dry and warm in a draft-free place. Make sure that the hay you give it has no weeds in it and is not moldy.

The droppings often tell you whether or not your pet is well. If these are not firm and dry, it probably means that your pet has an upset stomach. Check your pet's claws when you groom it, as they sometimes grow very long and need to be trimmed. Check its teeth as they may grow too long and need to be cut back by a vet.

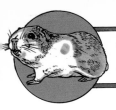

Finding out more

One of the interesting things about living creatures is that every one is different from all the others. If you study your pet you can discover the things that are special to it.

You will not need any very special equipment to study your guinea pig, though a ruler and a watch which marks seconds may be very helpful. It is a good idea to make a guinea pig diary. Always write down what you find out as it is very difficult to remember the details later.

▽ You should illustrate your guinea pig diary with sketches to show how your guinea pig does things. Even if you are not very good at drawing, you can show, for example, whether it sleeps curled up or stretched out. This can help make your project into a piece of real scientific research.

△ Once you start to watch your guinea pig you will find that rest is very important to it.

When you first get your guinea pig you can easily find out how fast it grows. Put it on a level surface and measure its length and its height every three days until you are certain that it has stopped growing. Find out if it grows at the same rate all the time. Measure the length of one of its hind feet and see if this grows as much as the rest of its body.

Find out how much time it spends in feeding and what its favorite food is. See how long it spends each day in grooming, sunbathing or sleeping. If you have more than one guinea pig you can find out exactly how different they are.

▽ If your guinea pig has babies you can study the way she looks after them and how they change as they grow.

Index

PRINTED IN BELGIUM BY
proost
INTERNATIONAL BOOK PRODUCTION